Pink Pig

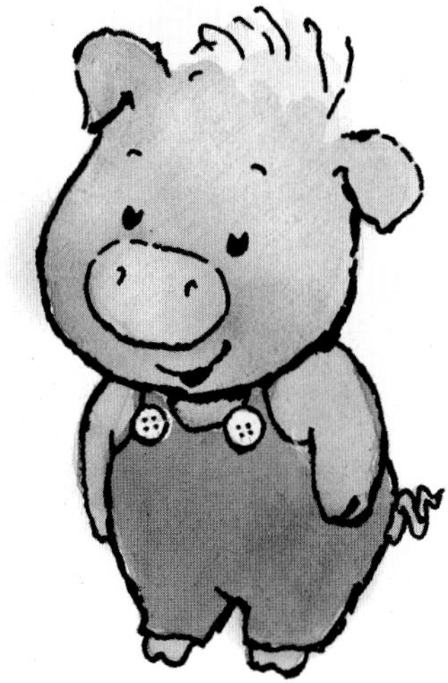

Written by Tim Anton
Illustrated by Sheila Lucas

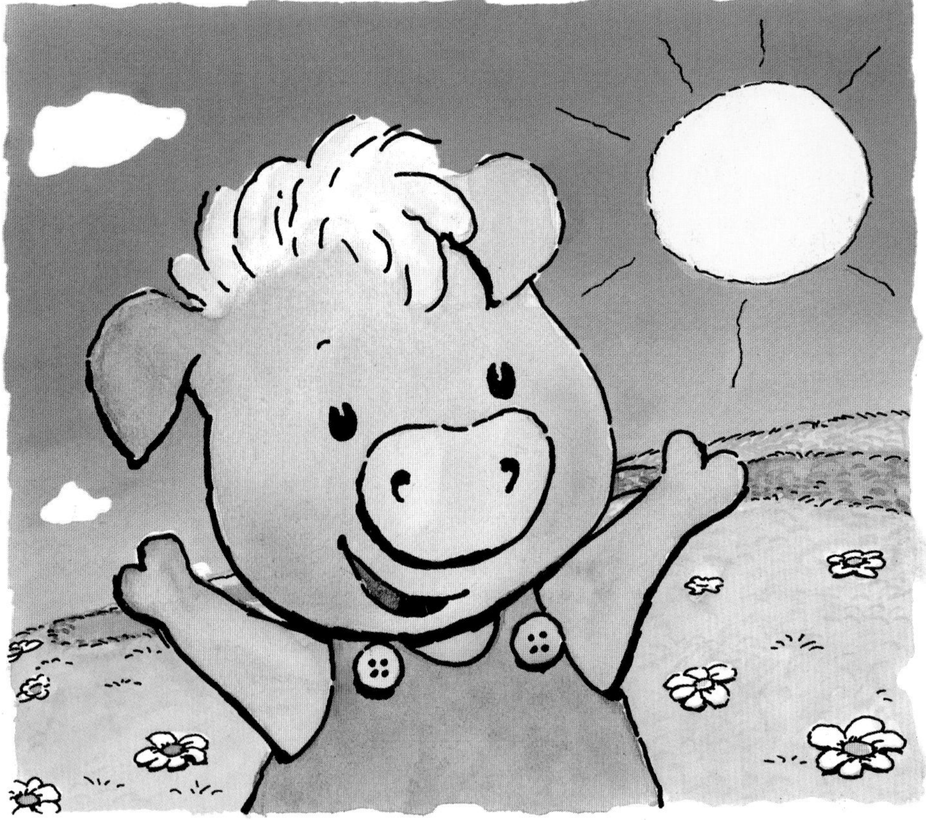

Pink pig, pink pig,

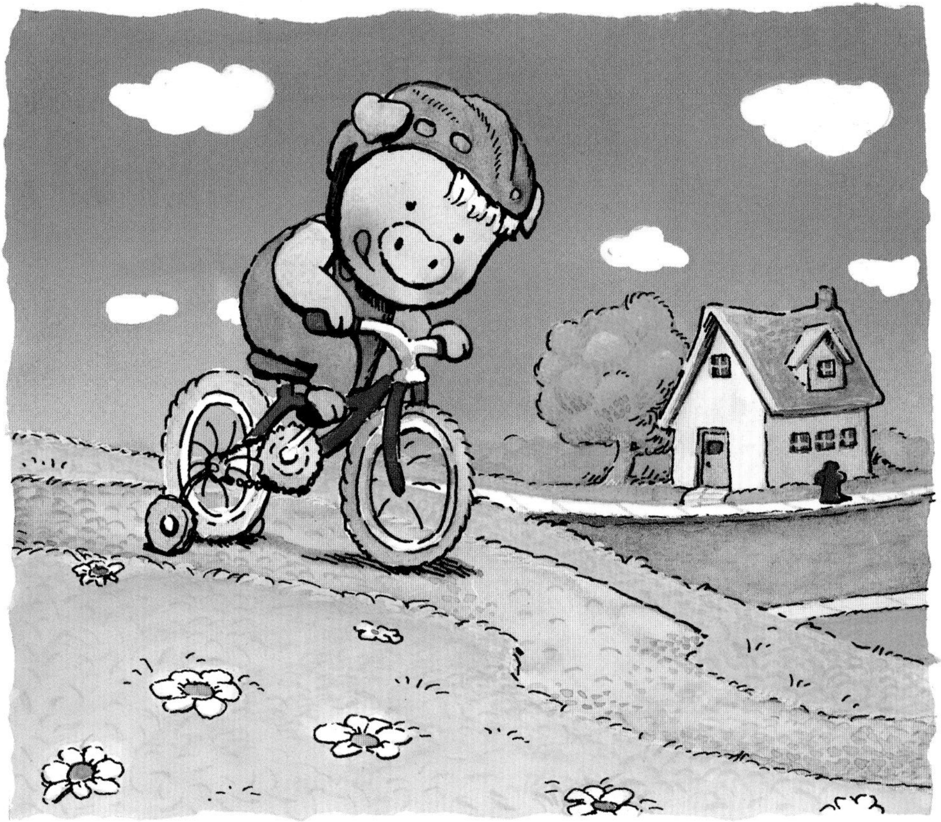

ride, ride, ride.

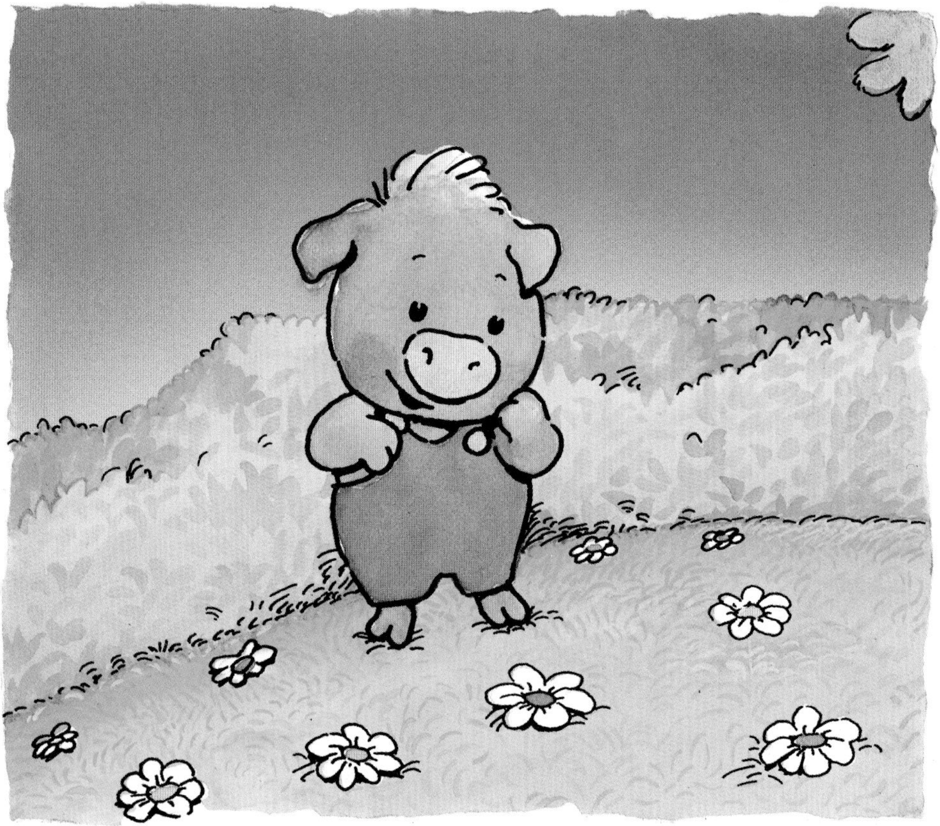

Pink pig, pink pig,

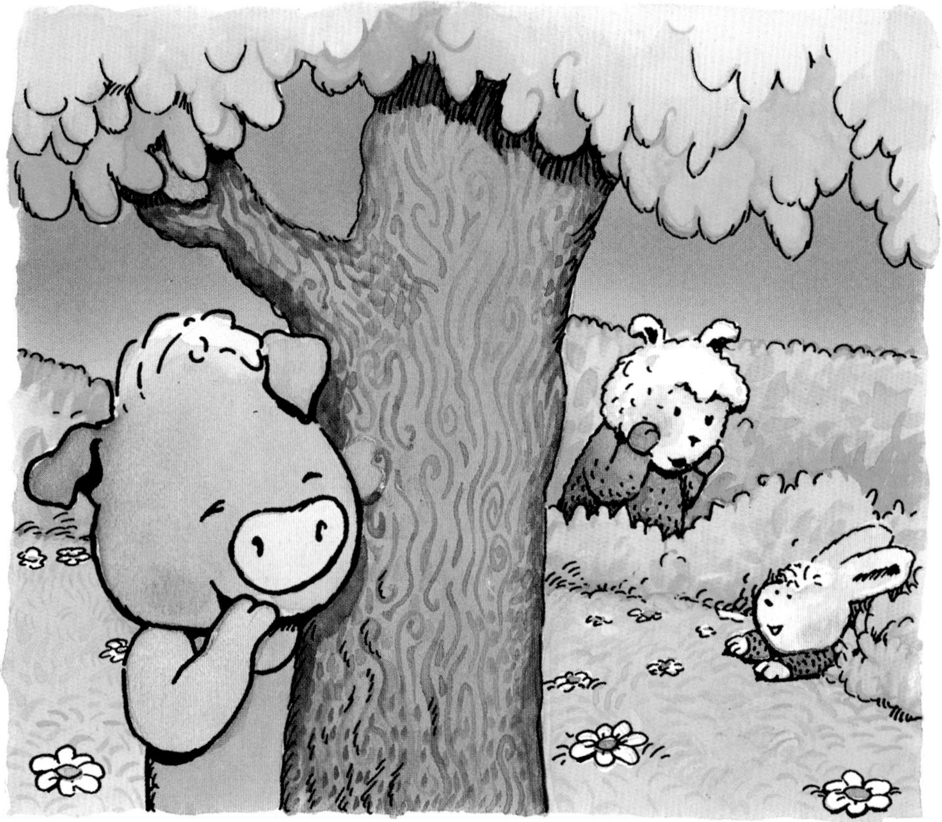

hide, hide, hide.

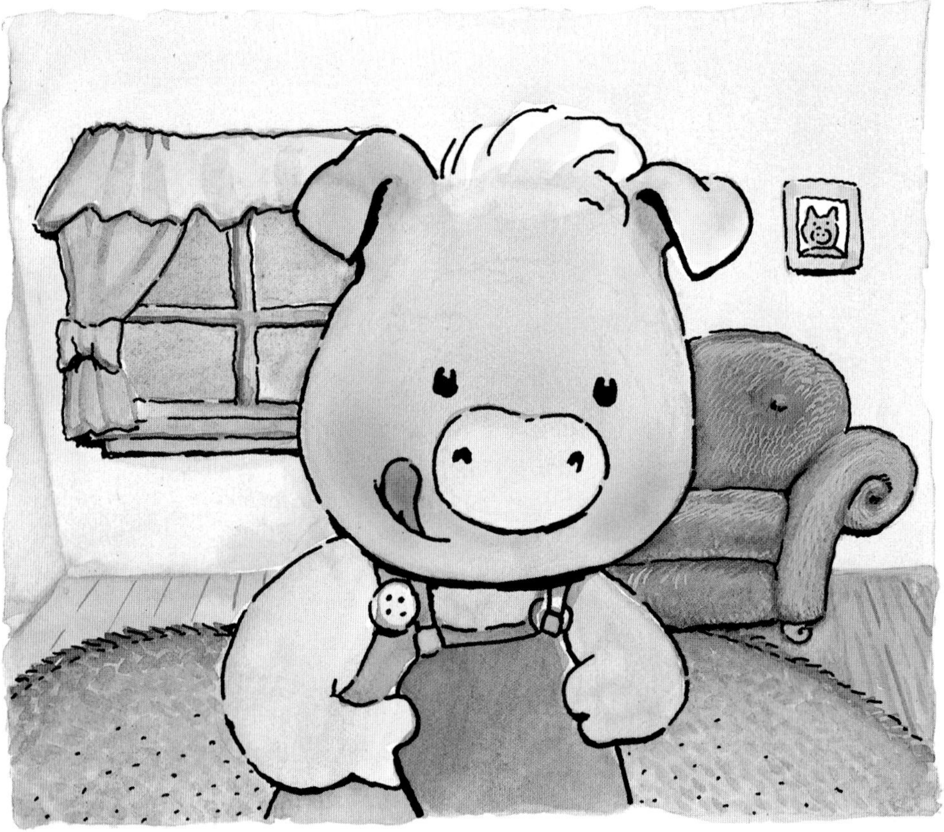

Pink pig, pink pig,

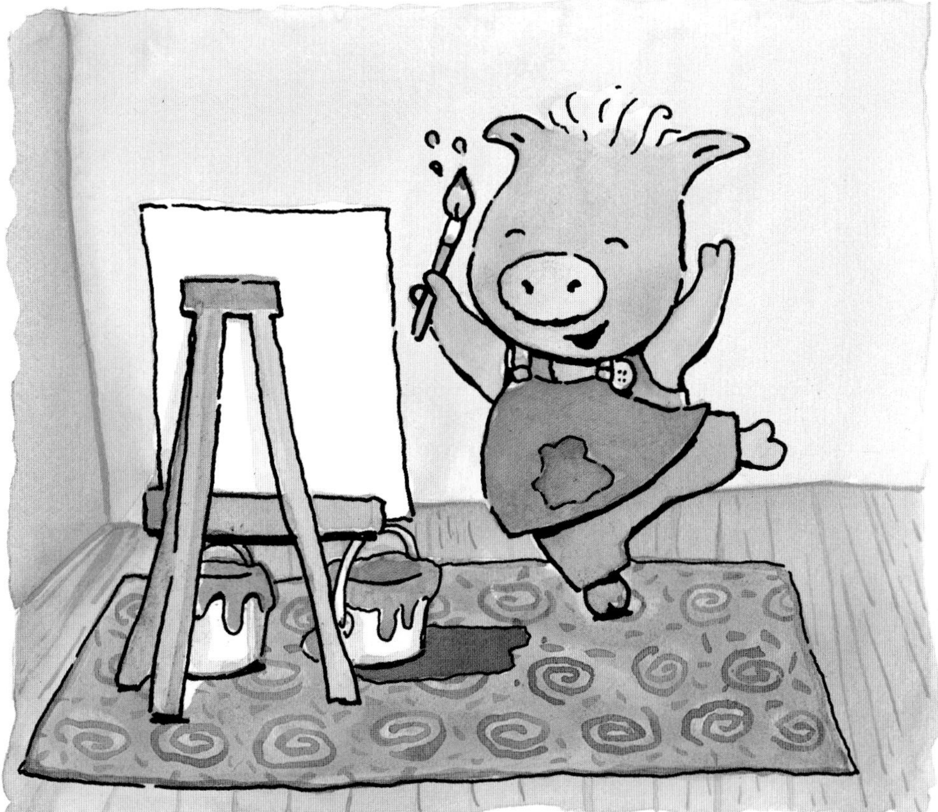

paint, paint, paint.

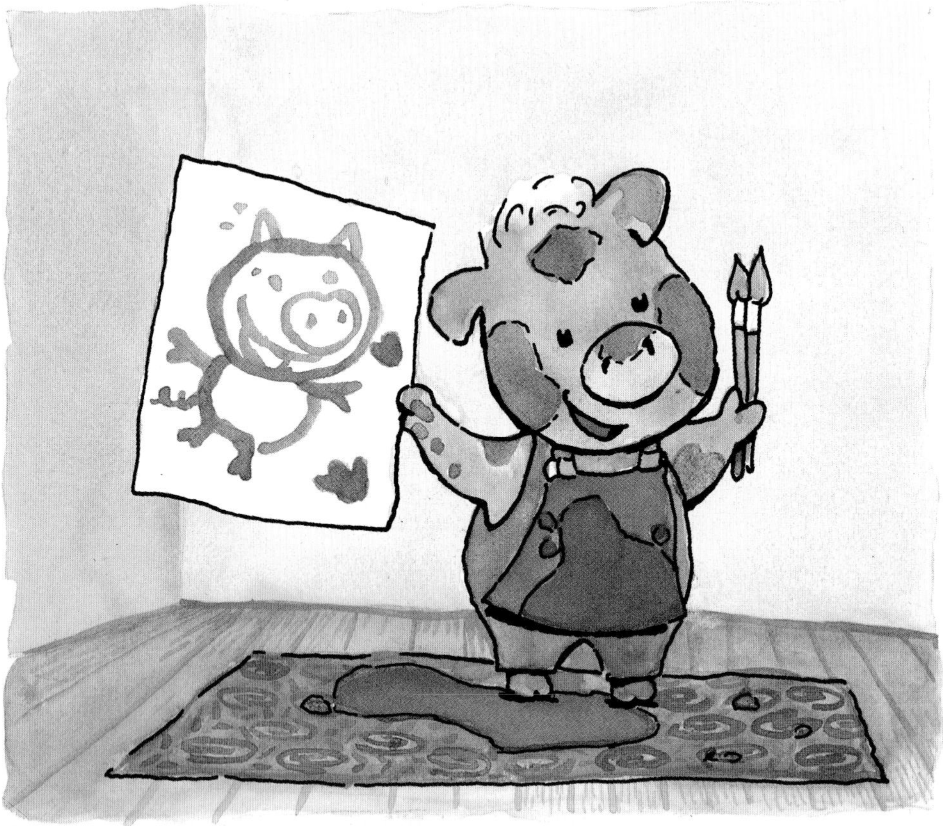

Purple pig!